MOTIVATION
BREAKS EVERY CHAIN

In this life we believe that motivation is universal!

Motivation has no color,

it has no statement to make

as to who is more than or less of!

There is no declaration of male or female!

I believe that motivation begins in the spirit,

deep within.

If we could understand

where we are spiritually

then we can make some positive moves

in the natural.

Enjoy the words within!

Let them inspire you,

encourage you

and move you to reach the full potential

that God has just for you!

Angel Ferguson

I dedicate this book to experience!

As it is & will forever be my teacher.

"To live is to learn, and I am still alive therefore I am forever learning"!

To my parents Apostle Namon Wilson Jr. & Pastor Valerie L. Wilson.

Years ago as I sat in the pews of

Charity Lighthouse of Faith Inc., (my parents ministry)

and I would write as my father would minister and teach

I had no idea that this was my path!

I love them so very dearly and cherish all that they have instilled in me.

To my children and granddaughter,

always reminding me of who I am first, Mom & Nanna.

I love you all,

Angel L Ferguson

All rights reserved

Including the right to reproduce this book

or portions thereof in any form whatsoever.

For information, address

Angel Ferguson's WordProcessing

8034 of the Americas, Tampa, FL 33617

Copyright * 2014 by Angel Ferguson

a trustee of

HOPE & TRUTH MAGAZINE

All Rights Reserved

Published in the United States

By Angel Ferguson's WordProcessing, FL

WWW.ANGELFERGUSONSWORDPROCESSING.COM

Printed in the United States

Author Angel Ferguson

Book Cover Design By: James Ferguson III

Artwork James Ferguson III

Editor Angel Ferguson

Assistant Editor Rebecca Wilson

WORKS BY ANGEL FERGUSON

HOPE & TRUTH MAGAZINE

WORDS, THOUGHTS & INSPIRATIONS

THE SOUL OF A WOMAN & HER TIME

ROAD MAP TO SELF-PUBLISHING

MORNING INSPIRATIONS

CONTRIBUTING POET WITH POETRY.COM

CONTRIBUTING POET WITH AUTHORSLOVEQUOTES.COM

CONTRIBUTING WRITER WITH WRITERS QUOTES.COM

CUSTOMIZED GREETING CARDS

BOOK MARKS

JOURNEY (Releasing Winter 2015)

Morning Inspirations

So very grateful for this blessed day!

Before I can think to complain

I must admit I am blessed

to handle the task at hand.

Never complain

about the extra

laid at your feet,

it's a test to see if you can handle more.

Removing the limits!...

The reality is I am growing into me.

I am becoming me.

The more I write,

the more I look to inspire

and encourage others the more I notice me.

The more I notice the areas that I need to improve in.

I want to be as I say to be!

I want to be free to understand me.

I want to know my value and not give it away.

I am learning me. I am daring to dream.

I am allowing my dreams to live.

I am learning to notice distractions.

Yet, I am learning how to react to my distractions.

Is this easy? No

But how can I encourage, inspire, say step out in faith

and let nothing hinder you

if I stand still and let my desires pass me by?

How can I say "I wouldn't take that", if I accept it all?

I am learning to appreciate me.

Learning to say I am proud of me.

I am learning when to share and when to hold back.

I am learning my surroundings.

There is caution in the wind!

One thing has not changed, a desire to remain humble.

Morning Inspirations

Taking a moment

to observe the corners of my life,

it is when we focus

only on the things we can see & touch

that we tend to miss the things that has hindered our growth.

Just A Thought

As we grow in maturity,

It is the measure of our presence

that will make the difference.

Am I along for the ride

or equipped to lead the way?

Being careful of how we lead,

teaching those that follow

how to one day take the reins.

Stay encouraged, encouraging others along the way.

Morning inspirations

During this journey

I have come to realize

that unless I move with the flow of traffic,

I am at a standstill

I can dream,

scream,

talk

and the list can go on

but until I move from my seat,

until I walk out of my box

I shall remain limited.

This journey

is about together inspiring each other

and

I want to see you grow beyond the sky

I believe you can do it!

Let's do it together!

I am praying for your success.

Please don't let it pass us by.....

Morning inspirations

Life is good

if we invest positively into it.

Learn to Love past your pain.

There are better days ahead

if we would put our trust in God & push forward.

Do the unexpected, live!

Live & refuse to give up on you.

Stay forever blessed

Morning inspirations

We often sometimes

do not lack hope

we lack the action

to bringing that hope into reality.

How can I say

I have been cheated

or short changed

when I will not

put into action

that which I long for (hope for)?

Where is my faith?

I am the captain of my ship.

I put my trust in my guide (God) and I.

Morning inspirations

Let's take this day,

opportunity

as no other.

Time to reveal those goals & dreams!

Check your progress

not against mine

but against where you want to be.

Be encouraged.

What you didn't do yesterday,

take care of today

&

let's move forward.

Morning inspirations

Learning daily

that positive actions

Speak

Louder

than negative words!

Stay encouraged, encouraging others along the way.

Morning inspirations

Something to consider,

we look daily

to achieve

a certain amount of comfort for our families.

Learning

to take time out to appreciate the family we work hard for.

Putting God first means putting family first.

__Morning inspirations__

Something to share,

it's easy to settle

because no real effort is needed.

Yet it takes being tired of going nowhere

&

a determination

to pursue

that desire within to want more!

Your life is what you make it.

Morning inspirations

The thing about a journey,

you never travel alone

but by those that have inspired you along the way.

Never

think

you've gotten to where you are on your own.

God had some

people waiting on the streets you had to pass!

Morning Inspirations

Striving to be a better me!

I saw my reflection within the actions of my children!

How can I urge to correct in them

that which I have and done myself?

If I am to encourage

change

and

remain that positive role model

I must practice

that which I teach

although

we see our reflections in the mirror,

the glare

often times can hide the blemishes

but the fruit of our seeds

produces a harvest

that will show all after the polish has been applied!

Stay encouraged! Encouraging others along the way!

Loving You Forever & A Day!

Morning Inspirations

Just an observation.

We are in a continuous circle

that does not have an effective

end because we fail to wait on the directions of God.

A journey is a path

that will lead us to & through

many experiences

but a circle will only have a repetitive scene.

Wait on God's direction & get started

on the journey created just for us.

There is nothing wrong

with feeling a little wind

and the sound of the rain,

we are as eagles,

strong and able to soar above the rumble.

A question, can you stand the storm?

Can you stand firm against the winds of doubt

that will come to shake your faith?

Can you remain confident in your purpose when all looks bleak?

I say YES!

Maturity tells me that this strong gust of wind is simply a test.

Maturity has taught me

to realize that I did not get here on sunny days alone.

That although I was in the storm,

I did not get wet!

Encouraging you to keep pressing!

I know it gets hard

but it is all apart of molding you into your destiny.

It's more than just another day,

it's another opportunity

to pour life into your dreams.

Morning Inspirations

Taking the time to appreciate who you are!

Thank You for allowing me to share my

Morning Inspirations with you.

Stay encourage, encouraging others along the way.

Enjoy this day showing love to your loved ones.

Morning Inspirations

Maturity

tells me that when you don't know exactly what to do

don't just stand & do nothing.

Stand & Praise!

Stand & Give Thanks

for All that has been & for what is to come.

And

the next thing

to do is give.

Give

when you are need yourself,

no matter what the need may be

it's a blessing to give,

expecting nothing in return

from whom you gave

but relying & putting

all your trust in God

Enjoy our day family loving you forever & a day.

Morning Inspirations

Something to share,

a part of growth,

is to accept yourself for who you are.

Once I accepted me,

I began to understand me

then I desired change in me!

It's true

we have no heaven or hell to put/ send anyone to.

But we can determine were we will end up!

Morning inspirations

Encouraging you

to hold on tight to your goals & dreams!

Surround yourself

with those that aren't afraid of supporting others.

One thing to learn,

remember & practice;

share what you've learned.

Pass the baton of knowledge.

Morning inspirations

Something very heavy on my heart

the choices we make.

Daily we are given a chance to decide

if we want to have a positive impact or a negative effect.

And how can one enable & become

a part of a negative impact

then point out that was their decision once all is exposed?

Please think of the consequences before you make a move.

Is the outcome you're facing worth it?

Praying for the minds of people!

Walking away from certain situations doesn't make you a coward;

it proves your level of maturity

Stay encouraged, encouraging others along the way.

Morning inspirations

When I woke up this morning,

this song was on my mind

"What God has for me is for me"

meaning dreams and goals.

Such true words

but I am also reminded

that I must want what he has for me

and I must go after what is for me.

What is meant for you is for you

but what are you doing to bring it into reality.

Just something for us all to think about today!

Morning inspirations

Encouraging each of you

to seek God's purpose for your life.

Understanding your destination

starting your journey

&

live your dreams.

My sister said it best, find your fruit and pick it!

Morning inspirations

Something to share,

if God looks beyond our faults

& can see our needs of salvation,

peace of mind,

love,

joy

etc.

Who are we to judge one another?

Who are we to point out the next persons stains of life?

Maturity says

Lord Do a new work in me,

so that I will know how to love & treat those around me.

Immaturity is still saying God let them feel my pain.

Let us grow together, leaving those immature nature's behind.

Stay encouraged. Encouraging others along the way.

Morning inspirations

Encouraging you to press forward today,

Every day is not easy.

Keeping your heart,

eyes & mind

on the better things ahead of you!

No need to dwell on the negative things of yesterday.

Nor should you entertain those that try & remind you of your past.

You are growing daily into maturity,

unique & precious

in the eyes of God.

Morning inspirations

Maturity tells me

that I can't get anywhere

or go as long

as I focus on the next individuals faults.

One thing I have come to understand.

There is a reason

why the mirror has a reflection and not just an open hole!

Praying daily that God will show me Angel, all of Angel!

We are equipped to encourage not to tare down.

Encourage one another with no hidden agenda.

Loving you forever and a day!

Morning inspirations

Encouraging you to move pass some hurdles!

Those hurdles that are holding you back

from getting to that next level of maturity,

those things that are blocking you

from returning from school,

pursuing your career of your own business.

Let's pray about it,

give God thanks

for equipping you to succeed & put knowledge into action.

Push past that stumbling block,

believe me it is removable!

But you've got to be willing to move it.

Morning inspirations

Learning daily

to become more aware of how I treat others.

I believe

that God will send others in our paths

just to see if we will really show love as we profess.

You will never know

who is being sent your way,

be careful not to dismiss your blessings.

As yet be wise in all things

waiting on Gods approval before making a move.

Stay encouraged while encouraging others.

__Morning Inspirations__

This is the day that the Lord has made.

Let us rejoice and be glad in it.

No matter what,

rejoice.

We have been given another day,

another chance

to let God take control,

accept His council,

following His directions

as we grow into maturity

moving to the next level in our lives.

We are more than conquerors in Christ;

let nothing stand in your way of moving forward.

Stay encouraged,

you are beyond blessed & loved by the Most High.

Morning Inspirations

Appreciating these words.

"Learn not on your own understanding

but in all thy ways acknowledge Him."

Learning daily

to look beyond the surface

of what I thought I knew & understood.

Learning

that if we do not acknowledge Him,

We have no understanding!

I don't know about you

but I need an understanding of who I am,

why I am here

& where I am going!

Encouraging you to do the same,

Acknowledging Him

will shed some light on your purpose in life.

Loving you forever & a day family,

Morning Inspirations

Sending some encouragement your way,

Praying that you realize & reach your full potential!

I am praying that that your confidence is restored.

As long as we put Christ first,

putting into action

the directions He has given we can make it.

We have been equipped for the task,

don't take it for granted

or

it will pass you by.

Morning Inspirations

Giving thanks just for you today!

Appreciating each of you for who you are.

Encouraging you to fall in love

with you and the potential within,

Go after your dreams

like you breathe the air never stopping,

taking in what is for you

and

letting the pollution pass you by.

Enjoy your day.

Morning Inspirations

Encouraging each of you

too learn of yourselves.

Understanding who you are,

knowing your purpose in life

&

where you are heading.

Learning to walk in my destiny daily,

Here's a secret,

when we allow God to take control

He has a way of making His purpose for us

&

our dreams become as one!

Stay blessed & encouraged, you are highly favored.

Morning Inspirations

Sometimes

we must realize

that the things that come before us

are really not for us.

If I taught the lesson,

living by example

then it is up to the individual

to accept,

learn

&

utilize the lesson.

Leading by example has become my focus.

Loving you forever & a day,

Stay Blessed.

Morning Inspirations

Appreciating the moments

that make me stop & sit still.

It's my time to meditate,

take note of the things of Angel?

Make changes,

give thanks

&

move on.

Don't look at your alone time as boredom

but as a time to evaluate you.

Where you desire to be!

Morning Inspirations

Encouraging you to take that extra step today,

Push just a little bit harder today.

You are at the crossing for another level.

Truth is I am stepping & pushing with you.

This life is about teaching,

sharing

&

encouraging others.

To hold the experiences learned is selfish.

Encouraging you encourages me.

Let's encourage others along the way;

it really doesn't cost a thing!

Morning Inspirations

Something to share,

Maturity

says that if I have the ability

to travel the road

that will lead me to a better life,

why remain on the sidewalk of nowhere?

Never devalue your God given strengths,

abilities

&

desires.

Go after your dreams

knowing that you can overcome all obstacles

through Christ.

Enjoy your day.

Morning Inspirations

Learning daily;

that a lot of the obstacles faced today

are because of a lack of a solid foundation laid yesterday.

Learning to observe my every encounter,

have I faced this before?

How did I handle it?

Why is this situation back?

Maturity says

there was something I missed

&

until I learn & apply that lesson.

The scene will remain the same.

Morning Inspirations

Never underestimate

the purpose & power of an education,

it's essential for survival.

Planting seeds of learning now,

obtaining a degree,

a craft,

trade

so that you may earn an income.

Truth is

no one is going to bring you the silver spoon

or even put it in your mouth.

You have got to earn that spoon,

hold it yourself

&

make sure you can keep it.

Morning Inspirations

Only God

knows & understands

where you are.

Encouraging you

to stand still in His peace

until He directs you to move!

Never give up on you & the desires of your heart.

You are forever blessed & loved by the Most High.

Stay encouraged, encouraging other you encounter.

Morning Inspirations

Sending some encouragement your way!

Learning to put yourself in a position

to be blessed

& achieving your goals

by removing yourself

from the paths of negatively & doubt.

This journey starts

in the mind for an understanding

of your destination

then to you heart

(you must have a love for your dreams)

to stir a passion

to make it come to pass.

We come to encourage.

You must make it happen.

Morning Inspirations

Every day

of every moment

you deserve the very best

that God has to offer you.

Understand,

accept,

and

Appreciate

the person you've become.

I believe you have great potential,

don't allow anyone to tell you different.

You'll never know

what's in store for you unless you try,

your dreams are waiting on you to wake up & put them into action.

Stay encouraged.

Morning Inspirations

Change!

I am change;

I am learning to recognize the characteristics of me!

Maturity

has taught me to love you,

for who you are

appreciating the essence of you,

Not, trying to change you into what I need you to be,

But

for me to become who I've been destined to become.

Encouraging you to do the same

we cannot change anyone no matter how we try.

It's not that I rehearsed all the right words to say.

I've just learned

to listen to the music

&

understand the rhythm

before I decide to respond.

Morning Inspirations

Learning to appreciate people

for who they are

&

the purpose they have in my life.

No matter what!

We come to learn of & share with.

Some are for a lifetime,

some for a season

but never for no reason.

My purpose in your life

is to inspire you to learn of your purpose & destiny,

bringing your dreams into a reality

as we grown in maturity together!

Stay encouraged, encouraging others along the way.

Morning Inspirations

As a reminder

that as we grow & move

from level to level

it is important to pour the positive inspiration

we have gained into our households.

Love,

Inspire,

Encourage

&

Appreciate within first,

then spread abroad!

Continually learning

to point out the good in our loved ones

instead of focusing on the things we don't like.

As we have learned to do better, they will also!

Things to remember

Even God said "IN THE BEGINNING."

The finishing of the cake

is never done at the beginning;

we all must start from scratch!

Dare to dream,

moving with passion

&

progress keeping your focus on the end result.

<u>Morning Inspirations</u>

Life has an edit button,

each day we have a chance/choice to make it right.

Never be afraid

to pursue your dreams making them come into reality.

Morning Inspirations

Just a thought,

sometimes we need to slow down

&

listen to the rhythm

before moving to the beat.

Understanding what moves you

is vital instead of moving for everything!

Let's take this day by storm through faith.

Sharing some encouragement I just had with my son.

I see each day that we are granted to live

as a blank canvas.

You decide what colors to use

& the outcome

of your pictures.

Daily we have a choice

on what decisions to make.

Embrace your children,

instilling the knowledge & fear of God.

Be that true role model,

there is no reason for them to look outside the home.

Our children need us when they think they don't.

Loving you forever & a day!

During this journey,

I am faced with some questions on the daily.

As I've found the need to consider all things.

Here is a question for all of us.

Am I the driver of my destiny or am I along for the ride?

At some point

you must take the lead

of where you want to go

Or

become led where one would have you to be.

Know your purpose;

understand your vision,

never allowing anyone to tell you your dreams

before you've had a chance to wake up!

Morning Inspirations

Simply giving thanks for the life given to us.

Once we realize

our lives are what we put into them,

we can appreciate it all.

If we put nothing in we shall get nothing in return.

If we only understood just how precious

&

loved we are by God!

Every time you take a breath, that's love.

Just to live upon this earth is love!

Enjoy your day,

think of your blessings please never take life for granted.

Morning Inspirations

Encouraging you to keep your focus on your destiny,

It's not always about making the biggest statement

but the right impact!

We live, we learn & we grow.

Stay positive in all that you do.

Morning Inspirations

Just a reminder,

you are worth more than words could ever amount to!

You are precious in the sight of God,

never and I do mean never settle for less.

Smile

&

rejoice

as this is your moment,

your time to break the mold of negativity!

Enjoy your day, encouraging other along the way.

Morning Inspirations

Something to share,

without a doubt

every time I ask God

why something has not changed or happened

He reminds me.

He is waiting on me.

He has equipped me

for the task at hand

&

opened the door

all I have to do is walk in.

Let's stop taking our opportunities for granted!

Morning Inspirations

It is as simple as this.

You will never know if you don't try!

Step out in faith.

Use the potential granted unto you.

I believe in your potential

but you have to believe in you as well.

Stay encouraged,

we are so close to that next level.

Please don't give up or turn back now.

I believe you can make it!

Morning Inspirations

Embracing this new day

as a new challenge,

A challenge to do better than my yesterday!

What I settled for yesterday can't hold me today.

Being careful

to take care of what is now

so that I can handle what is to come.

It's a new day, embrace it with joy.

Something To Share,

Never complain

about the things you asked for.

God has supplied all your needs

&

has given you some of the desires of your heart.

To complain is to reject HIS gifts.

I am forever grateful for everything!

__Morning Inspirations__

Something to consider,

Sometimes

you have to step back

and review your current situations.

Am I controlling my life

or

is my life controlling me?

We all have a choice to decide our destination.

Daily as granted

we rise with another opportunity

to live pursuing our dreams

or

to let them remain untouched.

The choice is yours…..

Morning Inspirations

Wishing each of you a blessed day,

Enjoy your day.

Let your inspiration began at home then to one another

Morning Inspirations

May you have peace throughout your day?

No matter what it looks like,

you are more than a conqueror.

Hold your head up

&

smile,

Pray

&

praise your way through.

Failure is not an option when you keep God first!

Morning Inspirations

Your life

is your life;

it's your life

so live it!

Encouraging you to learn of your purpose & pursue your dreams, inspiring others along the way.

Morning Inspirations

Maturity says,

a part of growth & moving

to the next level

is too accept

who & where

you are

along

with a plan of action

With some positive changes!

It's a beautiful

day, take it in & enjoy it.

Morning Inspirations

Just a thought

Remembering when……!

Makes me grateful for…..

All that is in store for me!

Appreciate your past;

It is a part of the valuable person you've become.

Something To Share.

When my feet are unable to move,

I bend my knees in prayer waiting on His answers.

Morning Inspirations

Appreciate this day,

this moment,

this new opportunity

to make a fresh start,

make the next step

By

accomplishing one of your goals.

You can do all things through Christ.

Today is your day, let's make it happen together.

Morning Inspirations

Something to share,

Why should I complain

when I believe that God shall supply all of my needs?

We are equipped to succeed & not fail.

Encouraging you

to press beyond the past of giving up

&

make things happen in a positive way for yourself & your family.

Morning Inspirations

To each of you,

what God has for you is for you.

But you must accept,

trust

&

follow His lead

in receiving what is meant for you.

Enjoy your day Family.

Morning Inspirations

Sending some encouragement your way,

When you have realized

accepted

&

began to work,

live,

&

share your purpose in this life,

let nothing

or anyone

put a limit or hinder you!

As long as you

first believe

in the gifts

God gave you

all else will fall into place.

Enjoy your day.

Keep growing you are unlimited!

Just a thought.

Our goals

don't just happen

&

one day just show up

in a completed state.

We must start at the beginning,

creating each scene of our dreams!

Morning Inspirations

Loving the words of this song,

hopefully

it will cause you to stop complaining and be grateful.

'As I look around and I think things over,

All of my good days out weigh my bad days, I won't complain"

God has been good to me, I won't complain!

Stay encouraged, encouraging one another.

You are beyond blessed!

__Morning Inspirations__

Forever grateful for this new day!

Praying for the potential in you

You were created for a purpose,

get in tune with your destination

&

let the journey began.

Morning Inspirations

As there are no limits

to the sky

there are no limits

within you.

Let's set some reachable goals today.

Pray about it,

give thanks

&

make it happen.

Morning Inspirations

Just a thought,

When scenes becomes familiar

or had not changed,

It's because

we have not learned

the lessons before us!

Morning Inspirations

All things considered

needs time to grow!

Plant Well.

Enjoy your day

My Reality!

*Today I discovered why I could not breathe yesterday
I was trying to do it on my own.
I thought because I am now an adult
that I could carry myself
Go where I wanted
Taking care of my own needs.
But then there was this soft voice
yet as mighty as the wind
that reminded me that it is HE that has carried me
directed my feet
& supplied all my needs!
I thought my needs
were the natural things of this world.
He reminded me that my needs are life
breath, love, joy, peace, happiness,
long suffering, endurance, grace & mercy.*

Angel Ferguson………………………….

Morning Inspirations

Maturity has taught

me to ask

for the wisdom of God

so that I will not

rely on my own understanding.

Forever waiting on his directions,

learning

I can't ask Him to get in line with my plans

but to follow the plans

He has made for me.

Stay encouraged, encouraging others you encounter.

Morning Inspirations

Focusing on the positive this morning,

Never settle for less

when it comes to your family & dreams.

I believe you are full of potential,

value

&

you are blessed.

Stay encouraged,

you are so close to that positive change you've been seeking.

Morning Inspirations

Something to share.

Love,

encouragement

&

inspiration

should begin at home!

Make sure we are investing

in the potential

of

our households daily.

This is how you wake up a dream!

Morning Inspirations

Think not on what we have lost

but what we have gained!

Life,

integrity,

purpose,

wisdom

&

love.

We were created,

inspired,

encouraged,

and

moved.

By a foundation built on unconditional love.

Morning Inspirations

Encouraging you

to shake that thought

of giving up on you,

Look over how far you have come.

Don't turn back now;

you are a step closer to the next level.

Pray,

praise,

breathe

&

keep it moving forward.

Morning Inspirations

Maturity has taught me

to not honor life it's self

but,

The One

that grants me his life to live

that I might inspire

&

encourage those I encounter.

Cherishing the moments given to me.

__Morning Inspirations__

Just because

it didn't happen today

doesn't mean

there's no hope for tomorrow.

Morning Inspirations

Never take the moments

in your life for granted.

Cherish all

that you have the chance

to experience

as it has helped

to develop

the unique person you've become.

Morning Inspirations

Taking a moment

to remind you

to refresh your desires,

hopes

&

dreams,

Regroup,

focus

&

move forward.

Keep your eyes on what is ahead.

I believe

you can do whatever positive things

you set your heart's desire to do.

Let's keep growing together!

Inspire Someone Today.

Giving encouragement

to those you encounter.

Here's something I have learned,

it's a blessing to be a blessing.

We are a unique people

rising above any obstacle.

Enjoy your day.

__Morning Inspirations__

Forever learning

to stop

&

wait on the directions

meant for me.

Maturity has taught me

not to make a move

based on emotions

but upon the reality for me.

Morning Inspirations

If no one has told you lately,

you are greatly appreciated.

Thank you for being you.

You are beyond blessed & valuable.

God loves you

&

created you for a purpose.

You are worth

the very best this life has to offer.

Stop listening to those negative thoughts and words.

Focusing on the good

&

positive things that are coming your way!

Stay encouraged family.

This is your movement

your time

to live your dreams & goals.

Morning Inspirations

Something to share,

there is nothing like a new day.

A new day brings

about another opportunity

another chance

to make positive changes in our lives.

Welcome your new day

as a map,

only you can determine where you will go.

Stay encouraged;

never forget you are beyond blessed & valuable!

Morning Inspirations

Never underestimate

the power within you.

With a determined mind

& a master plan,

you can achieve your goals & dreams.

Let's take this day by storm focusing on all positive possibilities.

Morning Inspirations

Sending some encouragement your way,

No matter what the issue may be,

take it to the Lord in prayer.

Giving thanks & praise!

A secret I have learned,

when you are going through the trails

it is a blessing to give.

Yes, give when you are in need yourself.

Giving is not just monetary;

it is in your time.

Encouraging others etc.

Give & it shall be given unto you.

Morning Inspirations

Maturity has taught me

to appreciate everything that I encounter.

Life teaches us but what have we learned?

Never despise the test & trials.

It's a part of your training for better things.

Morning Inspirations

Sending some encouragement your way,

No matter what is going on around you,

don't lose focus on your destiny.

It's just a test;

you have come to far too turn back.

You are close to getting to the next level in your life.

Stay encouraged & inspired.

Morning Inspirations

You are truly amazing

&

one of a kind.

Created in the image of God,

He has a purpose just for you.

Simply become the best you that you can be.

Morning Inspirations

We can have a dream to become!

A desire to be!

And a talent that is!

Morning Inspirations

We are a great and valuable people.

We were never created

for defeat

but as conquerors

Rise above challenges before you.

As always

keep God first

in all that you do,

remain humble

&

He shall direct your path.

Morning Inspirations

Let us make the best of this day.

Focus on God,

allowing him to lead & direct your path.

Remember

you can do all things through Christ that strengthens you.

Your dreams

&

goals

are waiting on you to get them started!

Morning Inspirations

Forever grateful for another day,

Thank you Lord for loving us beyond our faults,

&

Accepting us as we are with no hidden agenda,

We are forever blessed.

Morning Inspirations

In this life

we go from level to level

become consistent where ever you go.

Don't become a stranger to yourself.

Morning Inspirations

Sometimes

hitting the brakes in life is not an option.

Keep pushing & pursuing your destination in full force!

Enjoy your day.

Morning Inspirations

I am encouraged to know

that our strengths are renewed daily.

Don't allow the set back of yesterday

to stop you today.

Continue to press forward towards your destination.

Morning Inspirations

In this life image is everything.

Watching the foot prints left behind!

While being careful not to step in the quick sand!

Morning Inspirations

An observation,

our trials come

that way we may be tested of our faith & maturity.

Until we can truly let go

of the past hurt

we & others have caused

that same test will keep coming around.

I encourage you to pray & ask God to remove hurt,

to do a change in you!

Renew your mind & all other thing will start to fall in place.

Morning Inspirations

Something to share,

even when the clouds come,

I am not overtaken

as I know who holds my heart,

my soul,

my hand.

I'm under the coverage

of the most High!

Morning Inspirations

Just thinking how fortunate I am.

Understanding that when I move on my own,

yes I will stumble

but when I give my way to God.

His grace carries me.

Lean on the One

who is strong enough

to hold

&

handle it all

&

will never let you fall.

Morning Inspirations

Encouraging you this morning

as you gather your plans & set your goals for the day,

Pray before you make a move.

Think before you speak,

have patience through the process

&

keep your focus on the prize.

I know you can do whatever you have set out to do,

if it's school, a job, a business.

You are beyond blessed.

Morning Inspirations

Sending this to each of you.

God has the final say in all things.

So today hold your head up,

things might look dim but the sun will shine again.

Change your thoughts

& think on positive things,

put a smile on your face.

Shake off that doubt,

giving thanks for what has been & what is to come.

I am a firm believer, it will get better.

But you have to make it happen.

Stay blessed.

Morning Inspirations

Something to share,

We keep running into the same scene

because we have failed to turn the channel.

Moving to another level begins with our state of mind.

What move me yesterday can't get my attention today!

Morning Inspirations

Something to share,

As we are making positive changes

and going after our goals

are we making room for these changes?

In order to accept

and welcome that newness

we must learn to let go

of the clutter

that's of no benefit to where we are headed.

This journey calls for learning,

letting go & moving on.

Letting go of doubt

low self-esteem

childish things

and grabbing hold of a positive mindset.

Enjoy life.

As always stay encouraged & encourage each other.

Morning Inspirations

Courtesy does not cost a thing!

It's priceless, give & it shall be given unto you!

Morning Inspirations

Instilling inspiration within your children,

We have some control

of this future generation

by the foundation we build.

So as we are striving

to do better,

we are setting examples

of what it really takes

to get from one level to the next.

Encourage education;

give then your interest & attention.

Help develop positive contributors of this society.

Morning Inspirations

Good morning, you are blessed beyond measure!

I will never stop saying this

as it I apart of me,

Appreciate who you are.

Never give up on your dreams,

goals

&

know your destiny in this life.

We all have a purpose;

I encourage you to take steps to bring your dream into reality.

Stay encouraged, encourage one another and just BE!

Morning Inspirations

Maturity has taught me

that when my words

seem to keep falling on deaf ears

to stop talking

step away

and just remain an example.

If our words & actions don't line up we are wasting time.

I can't tell you to run if all I do is walk!

Morning Inspirations

Learning to love through prayer

&

silence

instead of adding fuel to the fire.

Morning Inspirations

Fall in love with the potential of you.

Sometimes we have to become selfish

with our time,

attention,

efforts.

&

investments

in order to bring our dreams into a reality,

So today block that negative thought & conversation.

You have no time to gossip.

Move out of the way from that emotional baggage,

you have your own luggage to carry.

Set your agenda & goals for the day & make them happen.

Just A Thought

If I am too sail these seas

then I must obtain my degree as captain.

Not a ship made of hands

but of a sense of stability both mentally and emotionally.

For with a weak foundation,

I've allowed the holes to widen

and the liquid to drown my dreams.

I have gone to the bottom one to many times.

Before leaving my post

a trip to the lumber yard was my first mission.

Failing is not an option.

That lifetime has passed.

My direction as well as my assistance has become key,

no longer can I climb aboard

that which leans towards the quick sand of disbelief!

No time for games

or hide and seek,

please be real not with me

but with yourself in your endeavors.

I am not fond of waste.

A Reservation

Lost in a world when we want to appear deep,

surrounding oneself with books and people.

Trying to appear more educated,

dressing the part of perfection and of high accord.

I tried to appear rich

so I bought the things they had.

Speaking a language you know not the meaning of.

It was a purchase into their world.

Now I have all these things

and have seen so many faces

as I've learned so many names. But!

My shelves are filled with things

I have not read.

People I know nothing about,

a circle that I want out of.

I am a reservation awaiting

the good things that are coming my way.

I am reserved from the things

that I have learned to let go of.

I am, I am, I am reserved because

I have divorced my previous life.

I am, I am, I am reserved because

I have become engaged to another.

It is my value that is held near & dear.

It is me! That has discovered the value within!

I am, I am, I am crafted & created

in the likeness of the Most High!

I cannot be as you would like to fashion me but I am me!

A diamond put through the fire,

pulled through the coals

all for the refining of being me…………………………

As he has called me to be……………………………….

I am, I am, I am that music that plays so soft, yet rocks so loud.

O to be me is what I have destined to be…………………. just me.

So be you, that beautiful & precious you.

Created & crafted in the likeness of the Most High!

A diamond put through the fire, pulled through the coals all for the refining of being you……………..

As he has called you to be………………………………….just you!

Morning Inspirations

I dare not go back in time too undue that which I have become.

What shall I attempt is to take control of my present and future!

Yesterday we lived,

today we live,

As for tomorrow we shall seek life!

The fact is

that we cannot turn back the hands of time

when it comes to our past

but we do have the option

of

watching & controlling the clock of our present & future!

Wake up & let your dreams live!

Something To Share

As I face my journey,

I have learned to appreciate all that has & will come my way.

Just knowing that if God allowed it to come my way,

then He Knows

He has equipped me to handle it!

It's up to me to reveal what He has aught me……..

Simply appreciating this day and all that it has to offer.

Here is what I have learned,

I have come to accept all the doors whether opened or closed.

Especially the ones that were closed

because God knew that is was not meant for me………….

No need to pry & push your way in,

if it's for you the door will remain open.

Giving Expecting Nothing In Return

To accept your gift is not half as important as sharing it…………………

There is but one very important question

"whom did I impact today?

Whom did I help guide in the right direction

as they are on their journey of life?

The bottom line is not always about money,

it is about giving in those areas that one is not expecting to receive!

Something To Share……..

Maturity has taught me not to despise criticism

as it stops me from making errors

as I enter into the next level of my life!

We all have room for improvements.

Simply Because…………

As you are dreaming and pursuing, take time to notice the growth.

If you do not feel the need to make some corrections,

if you do not notice the change of your reactions,

if there is no desire to want more of this positive change in your life, then I say stop, step back

and evaluate your mission.

Go back to why you started it all in the first place.

And if you still are lost,

then maybe you followed the wrong path from the start!

Never lose sight of the why!

Let God take care of the when.

You just make sure you are prepared for the where!

Today I Realized

that although we are going in the same direction,

our walk is different.

Although our journeys are different

our destination is the same.

I have come to realize

that although we both speak,

the meaning of our words are meant to produce the same effect,

it is our methods that are different.

I'm not above or beneath.

We both crossed the road yet at a different pace

and took different steps!

Today I realized

that although the signal indicated it was time to pass,

our journey was not the same,

my feet took me through the white lines

yet you decided to cut across the lanes. Yet we both crossed the street.

Today I realized that you are me and I am you Just in a different form.

Christ created us all For the purpose of serving each other

Christ created us all To help our fellow man

He gave each a task on how he wants us to help each other.

He has given us all a task of speaking life

Building of character Being of peace

He has given us all the task
of looking to him for guidance in handling our task.

He has this plan that one plants One waters

But in the end only He can give the increase!

Simply put, I am proud of you and where you are in your journey.

I appreciate the love & support you have given me!

Thank you for inspiring me with your positive actions!

You are amazing!

A true jewel in His eyes!

Thank you, life for what you have taught me.

Thank you, experience for staying around.

Thank you, struggles for teaching me a lesson &

Thank you confidence for reminding me that I can handle it!

When there is no one but you,

and you are in the midst of where to go,

how to react,

and needing to know why,

stop, hold your peace and look to God!

I am here, I am waiting,

I need to know the next move to make.

He will never leave you nor forsake you.

You are His own,

He created you in the likeness of Him

therefore He knows just what you need.

Breathe & let God take control.

In closing, I pray that you have been inspired to learn of the potential within you.

It is now more than ever a time that we as a people should learn how to support and uplift each other rather than hold back and discourage.

We all have potential. I believe with the proper nurturing we can move mountains! It is so true, motivation has no color, creed or gender,

it is universal.

As I am learning daily to review each and every circumstance that comes my way as all things have a purpose.

And if God allowed it to come my way, there has to be a lesson somewhere that He wants me to learn.

As I often say, stay encouraged, encouraging others along the way!

Angel Ferguson is a mother, grandmother,

Small business owner,

As well as a published author.

With a compassion of inspiring others,

to learn of their talents and gifts ,

While pursing ones dreams & goals,

In 2012 Angel began writing Morning Inspirations.

As a newly established poet on several networks,

Writing has become a part of her everyday life.

"Without the guidance of God,

this dream would not have a life"

Angel Ferguson

www.ingramcontent.com/pod-product-compliance
Lightning Source LLC
Chambersburg PA
CBHW042304150426
43197CB00001B/4